My State OHIO

By Christina Earley

TABLE OF CONTENTS

A Crabtree Seedlings Book

Crabtree Publishing
crabtreebooks.com

School-to-Home Support for Caregivers and Teachers

This book helps children grow by letting them practice reading. Here are a few guiding questions to help the reader build his or her comprehension skills. Possible answers appear in red.

Before Reading:

- What do I know about Ohio?
    - *I know that Ohio is a state.*
    - *I know that Ohio is near Lake Erie.*
- What do I want to learn about Ohio?
    - *I want to learn which famous people were born in Ohio.*
    - *I want to learn what the state flag looks like.*

During Reading:

- What have I learned so far?
    - *I have learned that Columbus is the state capital of Ohio.*
    - *I have learned that Cuyahoga Valley has more than 900 kinds of plants.*
- I wonder why...
    - *I wonder why the state flower is the red carnation.*
    - *I wonder why Cleveland is known as the Forest City.*

After Reading:

- What did I learn about Ohio?
    - *I have learned that you can kayak on Lake Erie.*
    - *I have learned that the state animal is the white-tailed deer.*
- Read the book again and look for the glossary words.
    - *I see the word **capital** on page 6, and the word **kayak** on page 17. The other glossary words are found on pages 22 and 23.*

OHIO

I live in Cleveland. It is known as the Forest City.

My city is the home of the Rock and Roll Hall of Fame.

Ohio is in the midwestern United States. The **capital** is Columbus.

Fun Fact: Columbus is the largest city in Ohio.

The state animal is the white-tailed deer.

The red carnation
is the state flower.

We grow a lot of **buckeyes** in Ohio. Buckeyes are a type of nut.

Fun Fact: Ohio is called the Buckeye State.

My state flag has red and white stripes. There are 17 stars on it.

There are six national sports teams in Ohio.

I like to visit Cuyahoga Valley National Park. Sometimes we ride the train that travels through the park.

Fun Fact: Cuyahoga Valley has more than 900 different kinds of plants.

4241
4241
X R

I can see many different types of **aircraft** at the National Museum of the U.S. Air Force.

It is fun to **kayak** on Lake Erie from Ashtabula Harbor.

Filmmaker Steven Spielberg was born in Ohio. NBA **legend** LeBron James was also born in Ohio.

Fun Fact: Airplane inventor Orville Wright was born in Dayton, Ohio.

I can see grooves made by glaciers on Kelleys Island.

I enjoy going to Cedar Point amusement park with my family.

Glossary

aircraft (air-kraft): A machine, such as an airplane or helicopter, that flies through the air

buckeye (buk-ie): A brown nut, similar to a chestnut

capital (cap-ih-tuhl): The city or town where the government of a country, state, or province is located

filmmaker (fil-may-ker): A person who creates movies

kayak (kie-yak): A narrow boat that is pointed on both ends

legend (le-jihnd): A very famous person who is known for doing something well

Index

About the Author

Christina Earley lives in sunny South Florida with her husband and son. She enjoys traveling around the United States and learning about different historical places. Her hobbies include hiking, yoga, and baking.

Written by: Christina Earley
Designed and Illustrated by: Bobbie Houser
Series Development: James Earley
Proofreader: Melissa Boyce
Educational Consultant: Marie Lemke M.Ed.

Photographs:
Alamy: James Schwabel: p. 14-15; Images-USA: p. 16, 22; Tom Uhlman: p. 17, 23; Pictorial Press Ltd: p. 19
Shutterstock: Ronald E Grafe: cover; Kenneth Keifer: p. 3; f11photo: p. 4; f11photo: p. 5, 7; Volina: p. 6, 22; Michael Sean OLeary: p. 8; cooperr: p. 9; Nikolay Kurzenko: p. 10-11, 22; e.backlund: p. 11; railway fx: p. 12; Shout It Out Design: p. 13; Patrick Jennings: p. 14; Featureflash Photo Agency: p. 18 left, 23; Tinseltown: p. 18 right, 23; fisheradam13: p. 20; gg5795: p. 21

Crabtree Publishing

crabtreebooks.com 800-387-7650

Printed in the U.S.A./012023/CG20220815

Published in Canada
Crabtree Publishing
616 Welland Avenue
St. Catharines, Ontario
L2M 5V6

Published in the United States
Crabtree Publishing
347 Fifth Avenue
Suite 1402-145
New York, New York, 10016

Library and Archives Canada Cataloguing in Publication
Available at Library and Archives Canada

Library of Congress Cataloging-in-Publication Data
Available at the Library of Congress

Hardcover: 978-1-0396-9661-7
Paperback: 978-1-0396-9768-3
Ebook (pdf): 978-1-0396-9982-3
Epub: 978-1-0396-9875-8